Divine Order.
God's Way

Min. Pamela Nelms

WESTBOW
PRESS®
A DIVISION OF THOMAS NELSON
& ZONDERVAN

Scripture taken from the King James Version of the Bible.

WestBow Press books may be ordered through booksellers or by contacting:

WestBow Press
A Division of Thomas Nelson & Zondervan
1663 Liberty Drive
Bloomington, IN 47403
www.westbowpress.com
1 (866) 928-1240

ISBN: 978-1-5127-4632-7 (sc)
ISBN: 978-1-5127-4631-0 (e)

Library of Congress Control Number: 2016909848

Print information available on the last page.

WestBow Press rev. date: 06/24/2016

Contents

Introduction

After completing my morning devotion of listening to the National Prayer Everywhere call, I began to study and review several Sunday school lessons about God's judgment that came upon King Solomon's two sons—Jeroboam, who led the nation of Israel (Northern Kingdom) and Rehoboam, who led the nation of Judah (Southern Kingdom). My agitation at studying these expositions intensified the more I pondered them. It was disturbing at how all that sin and rebellion had taken place in that generation and how the people of God had allowed sin to increase and extend to future generations.

I thought they should have understood and joyously accepted the Word of God after all Jehovah God had done for them and was doing for them as His chosen people. I thought they would have listened to all their prophets' warnings and calls for repentance. Haggai had told them, "Consider your ways" (Haggai 1:5), and Amos and Micah had warned of impending doom, judgment, and captivity under heathen nations unless they repented of their evil ways and returned to God their Father; that should have pierced their hearts and minds deeply, but it did not!

There was little to no repentance in the land; the priests and leaders who were supposed to be the representatives of 'El Elyon, the most high God (Isaiah 28), were distorting God's teachings and leading His people far from His Word, will, and promises. They engaged in idolatry; they worshipped graven images, sacrificed their children to false gods, and encouraged others to do the same. They brought false worship into the sanctified place where only Jehovah was to preside and meet His people.

I condemned the ungratefulness, foolishness, and depravity of those who did these things and allowed them to happen. As a minister and a woman of God, I was grateful I did not live during those times. Our bishops, prophets, evangelists, pastors, ministers, teachers, and worshippers would never allow such a distortion of God's Word to occur today. We most definitely would not allow anybody to profane God's name in our presence. But the Spirit of the living God asks, "Really? Is that so?"

God said that this generation had surpassed all generations in sins and perversion, but we don't admit this truth because we are living in and are part of the issues. Sins, transgressions, and perversions dominate today among His people. Some churches have been established strictly for devil worship. The church has allowed many ungodly customs and traditions to infiltrate His church: this list includes legalized fornication (common-law marriage), legalized whore mongering (same-sex marriage), NAMBLA (men with boys), and sacrificing our children (prostitution, reality TV, Internet), and we indulge every desire (illicit sex, drugs, alcohol) and so much more.

God told me to write down what I tell you. Here it is. May it bless you as it has blessed me.

CHAPTER 1

Divine Order—Patent

I asked the Lord what I was to write, and He said, "Ye shall know the truth and the truth shall make you free" (John 8:32). Truth can be relative to one person and absolute to another based on their life experiences, knowledge, and faith. The core of any truth must be based on the origin or the definition of the truth.

To gain truth, we must go to the origins of all truth, God, who created the heaven and the earth. Nobody else has ever made such an emphatic declaration or was able to prove it. Everybody should agree on the research concerning ions and atomic particles out in space, but no one can claim ownership or even partnership in these creative works but God. Only God proclaimed,

> I am the first, and I am the last, and besides me there
> is no God ... Ye are even my witnesses. Is there a
> God beside me? Yea, there is no God: I know not
> any ... I am the Lord that maketh all things; that
> stretcheth forth the heavens alone; that spreadeth
> abroad the earth by myself. (Isaiah 44:6, 8, 24)

God spoke, and through His spoken Word, He created (*bārā'*)[1] all creation. This was His first patent, which also included the definition and the principles concerning it. *Webster's* tells us a patent is "an official document that confers and declares an exclusive right or privilege to an invention,"[2] which means anything and everything that comes after, pertains to, or is in regard to a patent are replicas, duplicates, or reproductions of it.

The Bible contains many proofs that God created everything and that His Word is truth. Moses said,

> Give ear, O ye heavens, and I will speak, and hear, O earth, the words of my mouth. My doctrine shall drop as the rain ... I will publish the name of the Lord: ascribe ye greatness unto our God. He is the Rock, his work is perfect: for all his ways are judgment: a God of truth and without iniquity, just and right is he. (Deuteronomy 32:1–4)

Daniel said, "I will show thee that which is noted in the Scripture of Truth" (Daniel 10:21), and the apostle John said, "In the beginning was the Word, and the Word was with God, and the Word was God" (John 1:1). John also stated that this same "word was made flesh and dwelt among us" (John 1:14), and he shared his conviction that "thy word is truth" (John 17:17).

---

[1] James Strong, *Strong's Exhaustive Concordance of the Bible*, Peabody, Massachusetts, (Hendrickson Publishers, 2007), 1479.

[2] *Merriam-Webster Dictionary*, New York, New York; (Pocket Book, 1974), 511.

So we can conclude that God is the truth, the Scriptures are the truth, and the Word is the truth. This means that God (Father), Jesus Christ (Word), and the Scriptures are definitive, established, truth concerning everything in life. Those who choose to misunderstand, disregard, alter, or refuse to believe God is the truth and the Creator of all fool only themselves: "The fool hath said in his heart, there is no God" (Psalm 14:1).

Since God made the only patent for creation, only He could set the terms of His patent, His divine order for creation.

CHAPTER 2

Divine Order—Creation

Now that we acknowledge that God established a divine order for His creation, we can gleam from this a few nuggets of wisdom concerning His purpose for His creation. "In the beginning God"; *'Elŏhīm*, a masculine noun that is plural in Hebrew, takes ownership for His majestic work. The triune Godhead comprises three distinct entities, each working as a unified whole with different roles; "The Lord our God is one Lord" (Deuteronomy 6:4).[3] All historical resources and biblical records denote that this unity is the Trinity of God the Father, God the Son (Jesus), and God the Holy Spirit and that they are equally God and had parts in the creative acts in the beginning.[4]

There are numerous Scriptures about God the Father: "Have we not all one father? Hath not one God created us" (Malachi 2:10; cf. Isaiah 42:5 and Revelation 4:11). God the Son, Jesus, had a part in creation: "which from the beginning of the world hath been hid in God, who created all things by Jesus Christ" (Ephesians

---

[3] *Strong's*, 1467.
[4] Spiros Zodhiates, *The Hebrew-Greek Key Study Bible*, 5th ed. Iowa Falls, Iowa; (World Bible Publishers, 1988), 2.

3:9; cf. Colossians 1:13–17, 2:9). God the Holy Spirit participated in the creation in the beginning: "The Spirit of God moved upon the face of the waters" (Genesis 1:2), and the "Spirit of them that walk therein" (Isaiah 42:5), and "My breath is in me, and the spirit of God is in my nostrils" (Job 27:3). The Holy Spirit is still a vital participant in creation.

The passage "And God said, let *us* make man in *our* image after *our* likeness" (Genesis 1:26; emphasis added) makes it clear the Father, the Son, and the Holy Spirit were all participants in creation. The apostle Paul is very certain regarding this: "The invisible things of him from the creation of the world are clearly seen being understood by the things that are made, even his eternal power and Godhead: so that they are without excuse" (Romans 1:20). And the apostle John wrote, "There are three that bear record in heaven, the Father, the Word and the Holy Ghost and these three are one" (1 John 5:7).

The Trinity was established as the patent of God in creation and remains the truth today. Jewish believers and those of different nations regard the number three as a complete and mystical number.[5] Because God has established His patent also for numbers, who are we to attempt to redefine that? Only arrogance, pride, madness, and folly would provoke any creation to rebel against the Creator. No one can overturn or amend any patents of God because God *is* the patent; He created just what He wanted.

My pastor, Bishop Sean F. Teal, always teaches that what is right about the first will be right about the rest.

---

[5] *The King James Bible*, Heritage Edition, Langley Park, Maryland; (International Bible, 1977), 87, 186.

CHAPTER 3

Divine Order—The Number Three

The number three is considered a complete, mystical number; from the beginning, it has signified divine completion, perfection, and unity (*tri*-nity).[6] God spoke into existence "the heavens, earth, and the waters" (Genesis 1:2), which make up all creation. God created entities in sets of three: the light, day, and night (Genesis 1:5) and the grass, the herb-yielding seed, and the fruit tree (Genesis 1:11). Everything is connected to God's patent of completeness: the sun, moon, and the stars (Genesis 1:14) and the cattle, the creeping things, and the beasts of the earth (Genesis 1:24).

Some other noteworthy patents of three include Noah's three sons: Shem, Ham, and Japheth (Genesis 10:1), whose offspring replenished the earth's population after the flood. Jewish believers celebrated three major feasts—the Passover, the Feast of the Tabernacle, and the Feast of the Pentecost. Sin is divided into three categories: the lusts of the flesh, the lusts of the eye, and the pride of life (1 John 3:15–17). So many passages of Scriptures

---

[6] *King James Bible*, 87,186.

contain references to three, including Amos 1:3, John 2:19, and 1 Corinthians 13:13.

God pronounced three curses before the flood: on the serpent in the Garden of Eden (Genesis 3:14), on the ground that humanity tills (Genesis 3:17), and on Cain (Genesis 4:11). Humanity was subject to three major judgments before the Abrahamic Covenant with God: it was expelled from the Garden of Eden (Genesis 3:22–24), subjected to the flood (Genesis 6–8), and scattered at the Tower of Babel (Genesis 11:1–9).[7]

Jonah was in the belly of the whale for three days (Jonah 1:17), and Jesus Christ was resurrected from the grave on the third day (Mark 8:31). The apostle John heralded patents of threes when Jesus declared, "I am Alpha and Omega, the beginning and the end, the first and the last" (Revelation 22:13). In addition, humanity was created with body, soul, and spirit. The number three is mystical, divine, complete, and perfect.

---

[7] Earl Radmacher, Ron Allen, H. Wayne House, *Nelson's Compact Bible Commentary*, Nashville, Tennessee; (Thomas Nelson Publishing, 2004), 6, 10.

CHAPTER 4

Divine Order—Humanity

God the Father, the Son, and the Holy Spirit worked as one to create humanity. "And God said" was the verbal command to create separately each entity of threes on different days.

However, on the sixth day, "and God said" was proclaimed twice. First, God created cattle, creeping things, and the beasts of the field, and then He created His patent for humanity. In God's patent for numbers, six is referred to as the number for humanity, which was created on the sixth day, and as opposed to the other creations that day, humanity alone was created in the image of God.

I was puzzled that man and woman, male and female, were not a trinity until God prompted me to read Genesis 1:27 again. I noticed the word *created* came up three times,[8] and I realized the last time the word *created* was mentioned was talking about the word *them*.

Something different was said on the third day; God said, "Let the earth bring forth grass, the herb yielding seed and the fruit tree

---

[8] Nelson, 2.

yielding fruit after his kind," but then, God added, "whose seed is in itself" (Genesis 1:11).

At the time of Adam's creation, God had already created the very first seed in itself and placed it in Adam; it became the first patented child. Neither Adam nor Eve, who had been created, could create by themselves, but Adam was the progeny for all seed, and Eve was the seed carrier who would give birth to the first child. All that was needed to keep humanity reproducing had already been perfected in Adam.

God's use of three is consistent throughout the creation week. Only a man and woman can produce a child; the Triune God— Father, Son and Holy Spirit—coexist as three in one; God created humanity as man, woman, and child (seed) in "His image and His Likeness" (Genesis 1:26).

The traditional view of humanity as bearing the image of God means it is to give evidence of God's moral, ethical, and intellectual views, but there is a physical as well as a spiritual concept concerning God's image and likeness. God formed humanity and "breathed into his nostrils the breath of life, and man became a living soul" (Genesis 2:7). According to the *Hebrew-Greek Key Study Bible*, the Jewish culture tended to view humanity as comprising only two parts—the soul and the body—which was intact at creation with the spirit ready to be activated the moment humanity acknowledges, accepts, and receives Jehovah as God. Note that sometimes they interchanged the words *soul* and *spirit*.

However, in the New Testament, humanity is considered tripartite: "I pray God your whole spirit and soul and body" (1 Thessalonians 5:23). The body is the "dust of the ground" (Genesis

2:7); the spirit is the affections, thinking and feeling; the soul is the heart, will, and consciousness. Because the words *soul* and *spirit* were so interchangeable, the Hebrew and the Greek were in agreement that because sin had cut off humanity's access to God, the only way it could receive salvation was for the Holy Spirit to open the door through Jesus Christ to regain access to God the Father.[9]

So let us see how such divine order, holiness, and unity become so corrupted and altered by sin that humanity could not then and cannot now comprehend just how far off it has strayed from God's plan for it.

---

[9] *Hebrew-Greek*, 2.

CHAPTER 5

Divine Order—Marriage

God bestowed His image and likeness on Adam, whom He put into a coma to produce Eve. Adam, the man (*'iysh*, the Hebrew masculine noun for male) was given a woman (*'ish shāh*, the Hebrew feminine noun for female)[10] for the covenant of marriage. The principle here was, "A man leave his father and his mother, and cleave unto his wife and they shall be made one flesh" (Genesis 2:24).

The first marriage was ordained by God; all marriages can consist of only one man and woman to this day. God's patent cannot be changed or voided, but people have tried to break the law, including and in particular the highest law, God's.

Scripture repeatedly confirms God's patent on marriage (Genesis 19:14; Exodus 21:3; Jeremiah 3:14); it is to be between male and female (Genesis 1:27), man (Genesis 1:26) and woman (Genesis 2:22, 23), husband (Genesis 3:6) and wife (Genesis 2:24).

Because God ordained this, we must follow His dictates to the letter. Also within the framework of the marriage covenant are the

---

[10] *Hebrew-Greek*, 1575, 1580.

duties of the husband, wife, and children to establish a godly home and family. Leviticus, Numbers, Deuteronomy, 1 Corinthians, Ephesians and numerous other books of the Bible speak of how earthly marriages should be.

The Bible deals with adultery, fornication, homosexuality, polygamy, bestiality, sodomy, and whore mongering, but you will never find any suggestion that God ordained these vices. There are indeed warnings and curses about participating in these vices because they are in violation of God's patent for marriage.

But too often, we forget or ignore the fact that marriage is a binding contract with spiritual connotations. Marriages between a man and a woman are synonymous with the relationship between the heavenly Bridegroom, Jesus Christ, and His bride, the church.

In *Kingdom Principles*, Myles Munroe wrote about "thy Kingdom come, thy will be done on earth as is in heaven." His book provides an excellent summary of how the earth is to reflect heaven for us to fulfill God's will for His creation.[11]

---

[11] Myles Munroe, *Kingdom Principles*, Shippensburg, Pennsylvania; (Destiny Image Publishers, Inc., 2006.)

CHAPTER 6

Divine Order—Covenants

God performed the first marriage and established it as a binding agreement between a man and a woman—a covenant, contract, alliance, or testament between two or more parties. The covenant of marriage is a reminder of how God in heaven communes with His creation on earth. God established the patent of marriage to reflect how He, the Bridegroom, chose to have a harmonious, loving relationship with His bride, the church.

But Adam and Eve, the first to be married, stained God's original patent. Ever since, humanity's relationship with God, family, work, community, and so on has been corrupted.

Adam's deliberate disobedience and sin (Romans 5:12) along with Eve's willful transgression (1 Timothy 2:14) had tragic repercussions we deal with even today. Sin severed our once-harmonious relationship with God in so many ways; it brought blame, disharmony, and discord between Adam and Eve, made humanity's work much more laborious (Genesis 3:17), brought physical death to all humanity (Genesis 3:19), and affected all generations: "By one man's disobedience many were made sinners" (Romans 5:19).

The devil's device of sin temporarily marred this relationship, and he tries to destroy the covenant of God. But it did not work then and won't work now because God sent judgment to "put enmity between thee and the woman, and between thy seed and her seed; it shall bruise thy head, and thou shalt bruise his heel" (Genesis 3:15).

We can see the effects of sin in Cain's murder of Abel, two people the Bible states as different from one another (Genesis 4:3–8). Abel sacrificed out of faithfulness, sincerity, and obedience to the criteria God set for offerings, while Cain's sacrifice was full of pride, insincerity, and disobedience to those criteria. God told Cain that if he did "well," God would "accept" his offering; but if he did not, it would amount only to "sin" (Genesis 4:7). Cain's desire to disobey God's way was evident in his negative attitude, lack of remorse, and disobedience to His commands concerning sacrifices. The creation can never tell the Creator how He can or should be revered and worshipped.

Sin's disastrous effects passed down from Adam to Cain to Noah and eventually to Abraham. God bestowed blessings on Abraham and his descendants (Genesis 22:18), who later became the nation of Israel. This covenant with Abraham extended through Isaac, Jacob, David, and each generation that came from Abraham's seed. The covenant declared that Jehovah God,

> thy maker is thine husband; the Lord of host is his
> name; and thy Redeemer the Holy One of Israel;
> the God of the whole earth shall He be called; for
> the Lord hath called thee as a woman forsaken and

grieved in spirit, and a <u>wife </u>of youth, when thou
wast refused, saith thy God. (Isaiah 54:5–6)

God's covenant with Abraham and Israel was to repair the
original, harmonious relationship between He and His creation
after sin in the Garden of Eden had caused severe separation.
The terms of the Abrahamic covenant that the prophet Moses
continued in were based on the Ten Commandments (Exodus
20:1–20), the laws of God. The first commandment set up the rest
of the law: "I am the Lord thy God" and "Thou shalt have no other
gods before me" (Exodus 20:2–3).

The Bible assures us that God the Creator never breaks His
covenant with His people; they will be blessed by God as long
as they keep covenant with Him, but they will be judged and
punished whenever they violate the covenant. The nation of Israel
sinned and provoked God "by profaning the covenant of our
fathers ... Judah hath profaned the holiness of the Lord which he
loved, and hath married the daughter of a strange god" (Malachi
2:10–11). The Israelites were repeatedly told throughout the Word
of God and by the prophets what they should not do to avoid
offending Him (Deuteronomy 7:3; Joshua 23:12; Nehemiah 13:23).

But Israel did not repair the covenant it had with God; it
also angered Him by trying to change His patent. The Israelites
substituted a new system for God's original patent with them,
His chosen people, when they started worshipping false gods.
Instead of the Israelites being God's bride, they distorted His
image with marriage to another bridegroom, Sodom (Genesis
18:20; Leviticus 18:22).

Israel's sins stained God's patents and covenants, but God always let them know how He felt about that through the prophets: "The Redeemer shall come to Zion and unto them that turn from transgression in Jacob, saith the Lord" (Isaiah 59:20). Isaiah also prophesied concerning the rod that would descend to King David through Abraham and Jesse that would lead to the holy seed, Christ, who was spoken of in God's judgment and curse on the devil in the Garden of Eden after the first sin had occurred.

The curse, *'ārar*, was placed on the devil and his seed (Genesis 3:14–15), and enmity was placed between him and the woman. This is still a battleground for the woman, but thanks be to God, we know how the victory was and still is being won. It is clear from that statement that the devil has as his offspring a "sinful nation, a people laden with iniquity, a seed of evildoers, children that are corrupter" (Isaiah 1:4). Their ways, customs and lifestyles mimic Cain's ways (John 8:44). A curse binds with a spell to hem in or render someone powerless to resist.[12] Curses exist today; they will work on and in all who walk in Cain's ways.

However, remember that Adam and Eve were not cursed by God. Only Satan the devil was cursed, which brings us to the nemesis, who is the victorious and triumphant one that was prophesied about as "her seed" (Genesis 3:15)—Jesus the Christ.

---

[12] *Hebrew-Greek*, 1580.

CHAPTER 7

Divine Order—Christ

God told Satan, "I will put enmity between thee and the woman, and between thy seed and her seed" (Genesis 3:15). The word *seed*, *zerà*, is a masculine noun that means sowing, plant, posterity, offspring, and at times male sperm, spêrma.[13] The fact that Abraham's seed (Israel) could not restore the original patent in creation is evident in what the apostle Paul wrote: "He saith not, and to seeds, as of many: but as of one, and to thy seed, which is Christ" (Galatians 3:16). So Jesus Christ was the fulfillment of the blessed covenant between God and Abraham.

Eve thought that her third son, Seth, was to be a replacement for Abel and a fulfillment for the promised "seed" (Genesis 3:15) when she said God "hath appointed me another seed" (Genesis 4:25). She grasped correctly only the minutest of divine insight into the fulfilling of that mysterious, prophetic, majestic, and marvelous revelation. She was correct concerning Seth, who physically replaced Abel, but Seth was only a son born out of the seed and in the likeness and the image of his human father, Adam

---

[13] *Hebrew-Greek*, 1590.

(Genesis 5:3), whose lineage could be traced down to Joseph from Abraham and David (Luke 3:38). Seth had a righteous seed; as the third son, his lineage was used to perfect and complete God's prophetic Word.

So now the mystery of "the woman ... her seed" (Genesis 3:15) needed some clarification because we all know women do not have seed. In the same way the phrase "her seed" was not speaking about Seth specifically, the phrase "the woman" was not speaking about Eve specifically. However, God created women to be His vessels to carry impregnated seed that produces new life. Therefore, when the "fullness of the time was come, God sent forth his Son made of woman" (Galatians 4:4).

God chose Mary, who "know not a man" (Luke 1:34), which fulfilled "the woman" prophesy. God impregnated her: "The Holy Ghost shall come upon thee, and the power of the Highest shall overshadow thee: therefore also that holy thing which shall be born of thee shall be called the Son of God" (Luke 1:35), "her seed." The Hebrew *yālad* means to birth, beget, labor, or a time of delivery concerning offspring. However, in Greek, begotten (*monogenês*) means sole, solo or only born.[14] Notice what biblical scholars called the immaculate conception is now referred to by modern scholars and scientists as artificial insemination. Mary was told by an angel of God concerning this only begotten child to "call his name Jesus" (Luke 1:31), and the word *begotten* is mentioned ten times in Scripture concerning Jesus Christ alone (Psalm 2:7; John 1:14, 18, 3:16, 18; Acts 13:33; Hebrews 1:5, 5:5; 1 John 4:9, 5:1).

---

[14] *Strong's*, 1508, 1649.

Though Abel was the original patent for holy seed and offspring, Abel was only a foreshadowing. Abel, *hebel* or *hābel* in Hebrew, speaks of something transitory and unsatisfactory; he was a temporary substitute.[15] We can surmises that Abraham offering up his son Isaac (Hebrews 11:17) was also a foreshadowing of the fulfillment of the prophecy given in the Garden of Eden (Genesis 3:15) until the only begotten Son was born and became the real, sinless, perfect, and permanent patent.

The patent involving Abel was made an acceptable offering (Genesis 4:4) to God, but Abel's offering did not restore the original, harmonious covenant relationship of unity that God had established at creation with humanity: "For if that first covenant had been faultless, then should no place have been sought for the second" (Hebrews 8:7). The first covenant, which consisted of the shedding of blood of animals for sin and trespass offerings for humanity, did not reconcile humanity and God because humanity kept on breaking the covenant.

God knew that would happen; He spoke of the daily animal sacrifices as being insufficient but as a "figure for the time … until the time of reformation" (Hebrews 9:9–10), after which God would make a better covenant with His people. This new covenant consists of Jesus Christ, the great High Priest, as well as the sacrificial Lamb of God so

> the pattern of things in the heavens should be
> purified … for Christ is not entered into the holy

---

[15] *Strong's*, 1489.

places made with hands, which are the figures of the true, but into heaven itself, now to appear in the presence of God for us. (Hebrews 9:23–24)

Jesus Christ, who was prophesied about from the beginning, repaired the covenant between humanity and God that Adam and Eve had corrupted. His shed blood established a legal testament that can never be broken. From the beginning, Adam's sin made it so that "in Adam all die" (1 Corinthians 15:22), but Jesus redeemed humanity by becoming "the first fruits … since by man came death, by man came also the resurrection of the dead" (1 Corinthians 15:20–21). Everyone who believes and receives Jesus Christ (Romans 10:9) is seen through the eyes of God's amazing grace and His mercy as replicas of the original patent because of the blood Jesus shed on Calvary.

Because of the enormous longitude and latitude of God's grace, all believers should be motivated to receive and walk in the abundance of God's grace and strive daily to live according to that grace: "If any man be in Christ, he is a new creature: old things are passed away: behold, all things are become new" (2 Corinthians 5:17).

Jesus Christ will forever be the only one who qualified to be the promised seed spoken of in Genesis in three ways. First, He is a descendant of King David out of the seed of Abraham as prophesied (Luke 1:55; 1 Timothy 2:4–5), and Jesus represents a type of son similar to Adam, our first spiritual earthly father (1 Corinthians 15:45). Second, similarly in type with Abel, "a keeper of sheep" (Genesis 4:2), who presented the first acceptable offering to God (Genesis 4:4), so also was Jesus the "good Shepherd" (John 10:11) God was pleased with. Third, Jesus' death on the cross as humanity's sacrifice "speaketh better things than that of Abel" (Hebrews 12:24) because He is the "only begotten Son" (John 1:18) of God, who "taketh away the first, that he may establish the second" (Hebrews 10:9) for eternity.

Through His birth, death, and resurrection, Jesus ratified this new covenant, and only He could put back into place the original patent for creation between heaven and earth and between God and humanity.

Chapter 8

Divine Order—Restoration

Jesus Christ, born of a virgin (Matthew 1:23), lived, died, and was resurrected on the third day (Luke 24:7) and became the head of the church, "which he hath purchased with his own blood" (Acts 20:28). Our eternal God desires to restore His original patent with a holy, unified marriage with His bride, the church, in this dispensation.

The finished work of Jesus on Calvary sanctified this covenant; it made it possible for God, the heavenly Bridegroom, to have a harmonious, loving relationship with His earthly bride-to-be, the church, through a covenant marriage. We are assured by the Word that God "hath made of one blood all nations of men for to dwell on all the face of the earth, and hath determined the times before appointed, and the bounds of their habitation," and He "commandeth all men everywhere to repent: Because he hath appointed a day, in which he will judge the world in righteousness by that man whom he hath ordained" (Acts 17:26, 30–31); He was referring to Jesus.

So let us review. God created His patent for divine order and His patent for the numerical order in the beginning of His creative works and acts. Jesus, one of the Trinity, came to earth and took a human body (John 1:14). He was crucified on Golgotha, later known as Calvary, and was buried on a Friday, the sixth day of the week, the same day of the week Adam had been born.

Jesus stayed in the grave on Saturday, the seventh day; the number seven denotes spiritual completeness (Genesis 2:2). He was raised from the dead on a Sunday, the first day of the week. However, Sunday also became the eighth day of the month in the creation of things, and that number usually denotes beginnings. We can choose the first scenario, wherein seven plus one signify the completion of sin being abolished, or the second scenario, in which eight signifies a beginning of the restoration of the original patent of creation. Either brought to fruition the restoration of God's patent of creation.

The Abrahamic covenant established this new beginning for Israel. King David was the youngest as well as the eighth son of Jesse (1 Samuel 17:12–14) out of the lineage of Abraham dating back to Seth. King David even acknowledged the preeminence of Jesus in the Scriptures with this verse that foreshadows Him for David: "The Lord said unto my Lord, sit thou on my right hand ... if David then call him Lord, how is he his son" (Matthew 22:44–45). This preparation for the restoration of the creation patent is consistent with the number eight, which denotes a new beginning. The church today chooses as its day of worship Resurrection Sunday because it reminds us of God's patent for divine order.

The covenant terms for the church are the Ten Commandments given to Israel, but they have been condensed into two: "Love the Lord thy God" and "Love thy neighbor as thyself" (Matthew 22:37–39).

Jesus loves His church, and He wants to sanctify it by His Word (Ephesians 5:25–26) so when He, the Bridegroom, comes back to claim His bride in marriage, He will find "a glorious church, not having spot, or wrinkle, or anything: but that it should be holy and without blemish" (Ephesians 5:27). The diagram below offers an excellent way for humanity to recognize God's patent and choose wisely which direction it wants to follow.

Father	+	Son	+	Holy Spirit	=		Divine Godhead (Trinity)
1	+	1	+	1	=	1	Absolute Singleness of Unity

Father	+	Son	+	Holy Spirit	=		Divine Godhead
1	+	1	+	1	=	3	Patent for Creation in Heaven

Man	+	Woman	+	Child (seed)	=		Divine Patent (Replica) for Earth
1	+	1	+	1	=	3	

Man	+	Man	=		Not Divine—Has Seed but No Ability to Reproduce
1	+	1	=	2	

Woman	+	Woman	=		Not Divine— Has Ability to Reproduce but No Seed
1	+	1	=	2	

We can see why the preparatory instructions called for the earthly replica of the creation patent to mandate that the husband is to love his wife, who has willingly submitted to him. This earthly replica in creation mirrors the heavenly patent in creation wherein Jesus Christ, the Bridegroom, is "the head of the Church," and He proved His love for them when He willingly gave His life so His church, His bride, would willingly be "subject unto" Him (Ephesians 5:23–24).

Every spiritual principle and command in Scripture came out of and is based on the concept of love because God is love (1 John 4:8). Because God so loves us and His church, He expects us, His children, to bestow love, grace, and mercy on others (1 John 4:11). We are charged to love one another as Christ loves us, and we are commanded to endeavor to work hard "to keep the unity of the Spirit in the bond of peace" (Ephesians 4:3).

CHAPTER 9

Divine Order—Repentance

To preserve the unity of the eternal Godhead in His church, we must avoid yesterday's pitfalls and traps. Having learned powerful lessons and examples from the beginning of creation, we can see how Adam and Eve's sin wrought devastation on them and their descendants. With all the written warnings and the constant reminders of the covenant, how can the church today find itself spliced into the ending of what can be called only a very bad movie we watch in living color daily?

The answer is found in the sin of pride. Humanity's desire to do whatever it pleases began in the garden when Adam and Eve chose to follow their own dictates rather than God's, which prompted His judgment and punishment. Almost every chapter in Judges alludes to the fact that "the children of Israel did evil in the sight of the Lord" (Judges 2:11) with the constant refrain, "Every man did that which was right in his own eyes" (Judges 21:25). People everywhere end up doing whatever they desire to do and with whomever they desire to do it with, but they must know sin will be punished.

Israel in general and the false prophets, priests, and leaders in particular left gigantic amounts of witness and testimony concerning the downfall, disgrace, and depravity that sinful practices and lifestyles can cause. King Solomon's son Jeroboam instituted his own way when he "made again of the lowest of the people priests of the high places: whosoever would, he consecrated him, and he became one of the priests of the high place" (1 Kings 13:33). This horrendous decision deviated from God's established Levitical priesthood and opened the door for many other false leaders and teachers and unholy priests and prophets. These ungodly machinations led to the mixing of false religious teachings and rituals. Sins such as fornication, prostitution (male and female), homosexuality, the sacrificing of children in fire, and many other vile practices began to take place in the places of worship for Jehovah the most high God. These actions provoked God's judgment and punishment on His chosen people, the Israelites.

The church today is struggling with sin and disobedience as had Israel, but there are now some new, turbulent, and challenging situations that have arisen. Every day, the prophesied "wars and rumours of wars" among nations and kingdoms along with the "famines, and pestilences, and earthquakes, in divers place" (Matthew 24:6–7) occur regularly.

Because "the love of many shall wax cold" (Matthew 24:12), we witness spouses killing each other for money. We hear of and are sometimes victims of terrorist actions, fratricide, racial disharmony, and discord between neighbors, coworkers, and nations. We emulate the actions of Israel and verify that "all the ways of a man are clean in his own eyes" (Proverbs 16:2). We continue to fulfill the prophecy concerning the last days, when "some shall depart from the faith, giving heed to seducing spirits, and doctrines of devils, speaking lies in hypocrisy: having their conscience seared with a hot iron, forbidding to marry" (1 Timothy 4:1–3), on and on.

We have become so arrogant and prideful that we have legislated deceitful laws. We have established precedence, added loopholes, and restructured guidelines so we can do as we please. We are attempting to create our own patents for life with our own rules and laws.

In *Kingdom Principles*, Myles Munroe wrote that the word *law* referred to two Greek words, *nomos* and *ethos*. Nomos refer to norms, that which has become normal, and "whatever becomes accepted as a norm in our society eventually becomes a <u>law</u> of our society. If we are exposed to a certain unaccustomed idea or behavior long enough, we eventually become so used to it that we start to accept it." After we accept it, we began to expect it and it "becomes in practical terms no different from a law, even if it is never formally established as legal statue." This is where ethos comes into play as the unwritten laws that are less formal than the "nomos," but those "customs quite often have a greater influence on people's behavior than any formal laws that are on the books."[16]

In the same way, Israel did whatsoever "was right in his own eyes" (Judges 21:25); now, the church wants to follow this same unprofitable, unholy, and destructive pattern. The church is no

---

[16] Munroe, 149–51.

longer just standing on bad and unholy principles that emanated from falsehood and lies; it is actively sliding down that same slippery slope into hostility and rebellion with opened eyes against God, His Word, and His Laws. Trying to create our own laws is asinine and preposterous; as Dr. Munroe wrote, we

> as a society could end up endorsing and normalizing evil or immorality. This is precisely what has happened and is happening in western culture with regard to such issues as homosexual rights, homosexual marriage, abortion rights, assisted suicide, embryonic stem cell research and the like. God's laws are designed to prevent us from accepting and normalizing evil and assigning it the force of law in our society" and "this is why sin and violation of the law never affect only the person or persons directly involved, but many others as well.[17]

We can do whatever we like as free agents in creation, but we cannot get away from the consequences of sin. *Nomē* is the feminine form of the Greek *nomos*; it means to pasture out or to feed out of (figuratively, the spreading of a gangrene, which, according to *Webster's*, is the dying of a part of the body due to interference with its nutrition).[18]

Kaiser Permanente's website says gangrene is a serious, life-threatening infection of the male genital area, the "seed" producing

---

[17] Ibid., 152–53.
[18] *Strong's*, 1651.

region God created to continue life. The second definition says that gangrene is the death and decay of tissue when the blood supply to that tissue is cut off leading to eventually the amputation of the dead tissue.

This simply means that those in the church of God, who "are members of his body, of his flesh, and of his bones" (Ephesians 5:30), are dying due to their desire to function on their own, away from the true source of all life, God.

CHAPTER 10

Divine Order—The Blessing

To continue to be blessed and favored by God, the church must comply with His Word, which denotes His will and desires. Jesus declared, "I am the true vine, and my Father is the husbandman" (John 15:1) and we the church "are the branches" (John 15:5). Jesus commanded believers in the church to abide in Him because there is life as well as rewards for those who obey His Word.

When God the Father, the husbandman, and Jesus, the vine, do not give the necessary nutrients to support the body due to its disobedience, the body is doomed to suffer gangrene and death.[19]

The reason for abiding as branches is to "bring forth more fruit" (John 15:1), but no fruit appears on a tree or a vine in a couple of days because it takes time for it to develop, cultivate, produce, and manufacture through abiding. Jesus said, "If a man abide not in me, he is cast forth as a branch, and is withered: and men gather them and cast them into the fire, and they are burned" (John 15:6). This pruning prevents them from sucking up nutrients

---

[19] *Strong's*, 47.

from the good fruit.[20] Abiding in the Word of God brings blessings; being severed from the vine brings death.

The Israelites agreed to the terms of their covenant with their Holy God wherein if they obeyed His commands, "All these blessings shall come on thee, and overtake thee" (Deuteronomy 28:2); but if they did not, "All these curses shall come upon thee, and overtake thee" (Deuteronomy 28:15). These curses came in a triad: famine, war, and pestilence (Deuteronomy 28:16–68).

Instead of obeying the Word of God, Israel provoked God to anger by profaning the temple, the sanctuary, and other places of worship with abominations, insincere rituals, and so many more vile and evil machinations.

Israel had forgotten what God had said to King Solomon when Solomon dedicated the first temple: "Now have I chosen and sanctified this house, that my name maybe there forever; and mine eyes and mine heart shall be there perpetually" (2 Chronicles 7:16). This was God's blessing on the sanctuary; if the Israelites obeyed His commandments, God said He would

> cast out of my sight, and make it to be a proverb and a byword among all nations. And this house, which is high, shall be an astonishment to everyone that passeth by it; so that he shall say, Why hath the Lord done thus unto this land, and unto this house? And it shall be answered, Because they forsook the Lord God of their fathers. (2 Chronicles 7:20–22)

---

[20] Nelson, 755.

The Old Testament closes with the readers having little to no doubt as to the plight and state of that nation.

God's charge to Israel to choose wisely (Deuteronomy 30:15) was given to them by the prophet Moses with "heaven and earth to record this day against you, that I have set before you life and death, blessing and cursing: therefore choose life, that both thou and thy seed may live: That thou mayest love the Lord thy God, and that thou mayest obey his voice" (Deuteronomy 30:19–20). This charge is good for today; it is still in effect to every believer of God whether Jew (Israelite) or Gentile (Christian).

God's desire for us, whether Jew or Gentile, is to repent of our own ideas of how and what we think should be because "the way of man is not in himself: it is not in man that walketh to direct his steps" (Jeremiah 10:23). As long as we live according to our own whims, we will see the fulfillment of prophetic signs and warnings concerning the last days. We will witness and see those who are "disobedient to parents, unthankful, unholy … Having a form of godliness, but denying the power thereof … Ever learning, and never able to come to the knowledge of the truth" (2 Timothy 3:1–7).

Believers in God are to "study to show thyself approved unto God, a workman that needeth not to be ashamed, rightly dividing the word of truth" (2 Timothy 2:15). If we allow societal whims, political factions, government edicts, and other religious tolerances to overshadow the unchangeable Word of God, we will be smack in the middle of the prophecy that depicts the last days with "all unrighteousness, fornication, wickedness … haters of God … covenant breakers, without natural affection … who knowing the judgment of God, that they which commit such things are worthy of death, not only do the same, but have pleasure in them that do them" (Romans 1:29–32).

Is this a call for all believers of God to kill those who participate in such sin? Absolutely not; this is a call for believers to strive to live according to God's principles and mandates, "denying ungodliness and worldly lusts [and] live soberly, righteously and godly in this present world" (Titus 2:12).

This is a loud call to all bishops, pastors, preachers, teachers, and evangelists to return to life- altering preaching and soul-saving teaching in the Word of God wherein we are charged to "reprove, rebuke, exhort with all longsuffering and doctrine" (2 Timothy 4:2). While ministering in the Word of God, we cannot afford to become distracted from doing so. We will end up wasting valuable time when we deviate from our ordained assignments by arguing about others' sexuality, rights, and so on. Anybody who wants to know the truth can find it in the Word of God: "He that cometh to God must believe that he is, and that he is a rewarder of them that diligently seek him" (Hebrews 11:6). Anyone can argue with another about the Word of God, but I dare anyone to present that same argument to the Living God.

Every blessing is predicated on receiving, obeying, and applying the Word of God; likewise, every curse is based on the rejection of the Word of God. All the power is in the Word; the power is the Word.

Doxology

Because all power resides in the Word of God, we, the creation, have to honor the design, desires, and the demands of our Creator if we want to receive His blessings.

No pastor, preacher, teacher, or speaker is eloquent enough to draw others to salvation except through the power of the Holy Spirit and the Word of God. No one can beat sin out of another; no one can rent out times of holiness because Adam and Eve's sin has come down on all of us (1 Corinthians 15:21–23). It is only because "of the Lord's mercies that we are not consumed, because his compassions fail not … are new every morning" (Lamentations 3:22–23).

We cannot buy blessings from a university, a governmental agency, or a megachurch. Everything God desires for His creation must come from Him. Though God has given us the right to do whatever we desire, even if it is sinful and violates His Word, we do not have the right to decide for ourselves the consequences for our sin; that decision is God's alone.

God will restore His divine order and a harmonious, loving relationship with His earthly creation. The heavenly Bridegroom will come for His earthly bride, the church, through "the marriage of the Lamb … Blessed are they which are called unto the marriage supper of the Lamb" (Revelation 19:7, 9). This marriage ceremony will bring about "a new heaven and a new earth for the first heaven and the first earth were passed away; and there was no more sea" (Revelation 21:1). The prophecy declares hearing "a great voice out of heaven saying, Behold, the tabernacle of God is with man, and he will dwell with them, and they shall be his people, and God himself shall be with them, and be their God" (Revelation 21:3).

This prophetic word is given in chapter 21, which is seven—the number of divine completion—times three—which signifies divine perfection and unity. The verse is also the number three as if to place emphasis on all creation that the original patent for creation is perfect. The attempt to restore the original patent through Israel was God's way of showing us why no human could or would ratify this covenant; only Jesus could do that.

God created Adam from the earth and made him "a living soul" in a spiritual body (1 Corinthians 15:44–47). He also created the second Adam, Jesus, "a quickening spirit" (1 Corinthians 15:45). Adam, "the son of God" (Luke 3:38), was named so because of the special creation. Adam's first son, Cain, rejected the way of God, but Abel followed it. Abel's death preceded the arrival of the true Son of Man, Jesus, the only begotten Son of God (Mark 1:1; 2 Corinthians 1:19; 1 John 4:15); the "second man is the Lord from heaven" (1 Corinthians 15:47). Jesus has always been the only one who can proclaim He is the true Son of God.

The matter is simple: we can accept God, His Word, and His Way, or we can follow our own paths. The grace, mercy, and loving kindness of God has always been extended to those who accept eternal life in God on His terms. But this same grace, mercy, and loving kindness will not be extended in some situations when we cross God's boundaries to satisfy our fleshly desires. We must prepare to meet our God and know the choices we make and the way we live will determine where we will spend eternity.

So choose wisely—life or death, God's way or the devil's way, heaven or hell. Adopt God's divine order for your life, for "Now unto him that is able to keep you from falling, and to present you faultless before the presence of his glory with exceeding joy. To the only wise God our Saviour, be glory and majesty, dominion and power, both now and ever. Amen" (Jude 1:24–25).

Printed in the United States
By Bookmasters